I0818424

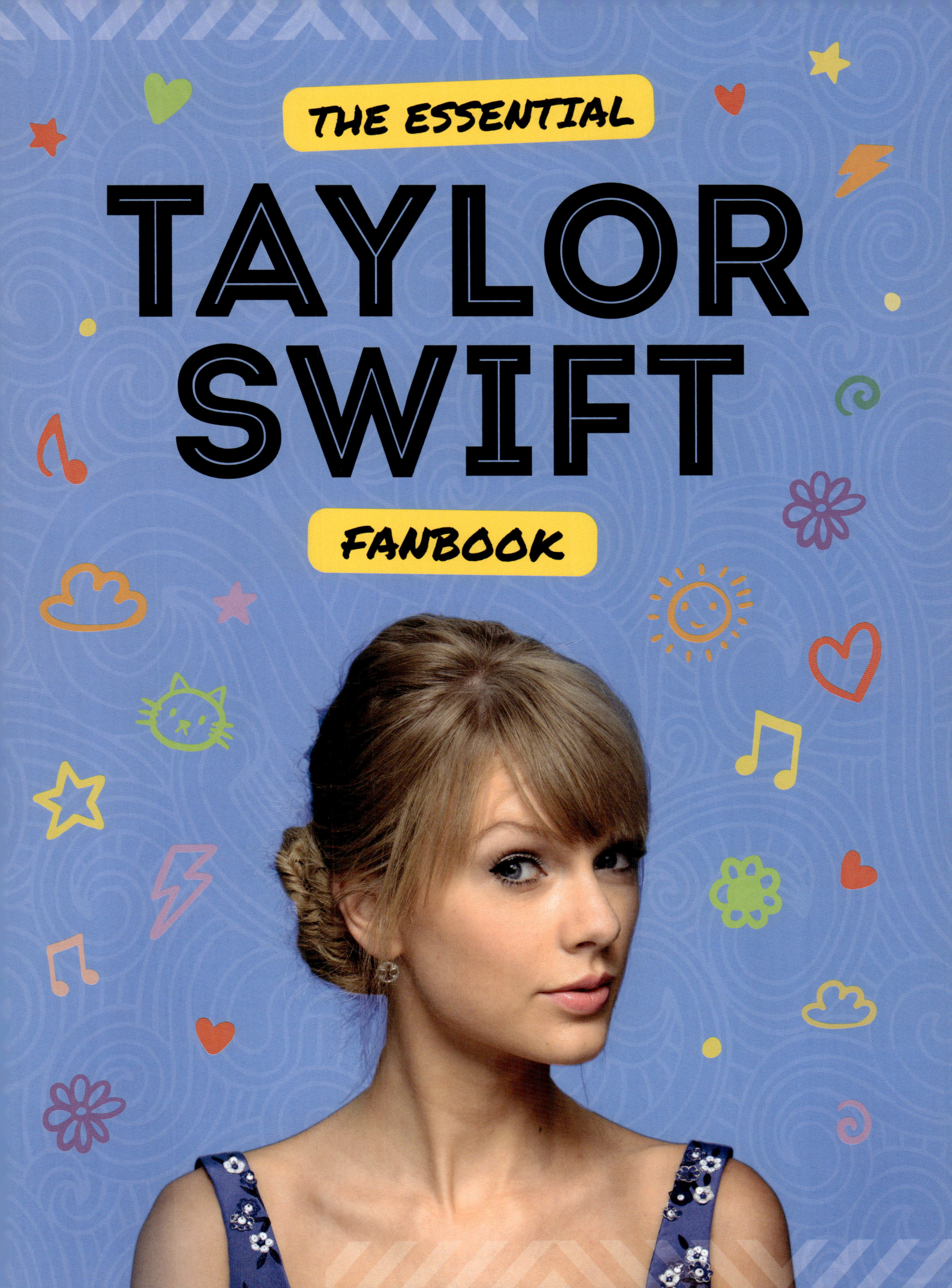
THE ESSENTIAL
TAYLOR
SWIFT
FANBOOK

WELBECK
CHILDREN'S BOOKS

First published in 2023 by Welbeck Children's Ltd
This edition published by Welbeck Children's Books
An imprint of Hachette Children's Group

All information correct as of October 2025.

The publishers would like to thank the following sources for their kind permission to reproduce the pictures in this book.

GETTY IMAGES: Axelle/Bauer-Griffin/FilmMagic 33BR, 54; Isaac Brekken 44-45; Megan Briggs 36C; Larry Busacca 1, 30TR, 32BR, 49TR; Gareth Cattermole/TAS 28-29B; Michael Caulfield/AMA 39; Erin Clark/The Boston Globe 26R; DAMEBK/Bauer-Griffin/GC Images 24TL; Rick Diamond 28; Rick Diamond/ACM 6TL; Nina Dietzel 8BL; Kevork Djansezian 41TL; Jeremy Drey/Media News Group/Reading Eagle 11TR; Francois Durand 48BL; David Eulitt 36B; Feature China/Future Publishing 42-43; Rich Fury 18-19; Jesse D Garrabrant/NBAE 8R; Bruce Glikas/FilmMagic 41BL; Steve Granitz/WireImage 38; Raymond Hall/GC Images 6BL, 23L; Frazer Harrison 32BC, 34R; Frazer Harrison/ACMA 40BR; Anthony Harvey 48BR; Taylor Hill/FilmMagic 33TR; Dimitrios Kambouris 52-53; Kevin Kane 10TR, 10BRL, 20-21; Kipuxa 22L; Pascal Kiszon 22C; Jon Kopaloff/FilmMagic 48TC; Jeff Kravitz/FilmMagic 9TR, 32BL, 33BC, 41TR, 60; Krissy Krummenacker/MediaNews Group/Reading Eagle 7; Dan MacMedan/WireImage 9BR; Maremagnum 10L; Kevin Mazur 15BL, 29, 33TC, 49BC, 49BR, 62; Kevin Mazur/TAS 24-25, 27; Kevin Mazur/WireImage 25TR, 30L, 31TR, 31BR, 41C, 56-57; Jamie McCarthy 33TL, 46-47; Emma McIntyre 49BL; Al Messerschmidt 48TL; Mark Metcalfe 50-51; Ethan Miller 35, 58-59; Neil Mockford/FilmMagic 32TR; Sarah Morris/FilmMagic 48-49; Cepi Nurdin/500px 22B; Christopher Polk 4-5, 40L, 55BR; Christopher Polk/ACMA BACK COVER, 6L, 48BC; Christopher Polk/FilmMagic 9L; Christopher Polk/Penske Media 16-17; Jun Sato/WireImage 29TL; John Shearer 12-13, 14L, 24BL, 25L; John Shearer/TAS 18-19; John Shearer/WireImage 30BR; Mindy Small/FilmMagic 55TR; Francis Specker/CBS 41BR; Amy Sussman 11BR; Brooke Sutton 2-3; Pierre Suu 31BL; TAS 11L; Valerie Terranova 15BR; Eric Thomas 37; Tristar Media 14C; Jeff Vespa/WireImage 40R; Andrew H Walker 22TL; Angela Weiss/AFP 33BL, 34BR, 63; Kevin Winter 24R, 48TR; Terry Wyatt 64

SHUTTERSTOCK: Olgsera 8BC; Startraks 23R

ALAMY: Album 26-27; Casey Flanigan/MediaPunch Inc FRONT COVER

Every effort has been made to acknowledge correctly and contact the source and/or copyright holder of each picture. Any unintentional errors or omissions will be corrected in future editions of this book.

ISBN 978 1 83955 332 5

Printed in Dongguan, China

10 9 8 7 6 5 4 3 2 1

Welbeck Children's Books
An imprint of Hachette Children's Group

Part of Hodder & Stoughton Limited
Carmelite House,
50 Victoria Embankment
London EC4Y 0DZ

An Hachette UK Company

www.hachette.co.uk
www.hachettechildrens.co.uk

FSC
www.fsc.org
MIX
Paper | Supporting responsible forestry
FSC® C104740

CONTENTS

Welcome

★★★★★★★★★★★★★★★★★★

Calling all Swifties! This book is bursting with all things Taylor, from fashion and fan guides, to cool collabs and her beloved cats. Besides learning fun facts and taking cool quizzes, you can hang out with Taylor's besties, relive her biggest anthems and melodies, plus try to tally the oodles of awards she's racking up. So, get ready to celebrate the queen of country-pop.

Meet Taylor

Do you call yourself a TayTay superfan? Whether you're a fully-fledged member of the Swifties or new to the party, this is your chance to get to know the gal behind some of the greatest hits in pop history.

MOM AND DAD

AUSTIN

OLIVIA BENSON

Swift Facts

NAME:	Taylor Alison Swift
FROM:	West Reading, Pennsylvania
DATE OF BIRTH:	December 13, 1989
HAIR COLOR:	Blonde
EYE COLOR:	Blue
STAR SIGN:	Sagittarius
MOM:	Andrea Gardner Swift
DAD:	Scott Kingsley Swift
YOUNGER BROTHER:	Austin Kingsley Swift
MUSICAL INSTRUMENTS:	Guitar, banjo, piano, ukulele
HOBBIES:	Making jam and baking
PET CATS:	Meredith Grey Olivia Benson Benjamin Button

As a little girl, Taylor grew up on her family's Christmas tree farm in Pennsylvania.

How It Started vs. How It's Going

From a wavy-haired, country-singing teen who came onto the scene in the early 2000s to a sensational superstar with sell-out stadium tours! This is Taylor's journey to stardom...

Taylor's Roots

Young Tay lived on a Christmas tree farm and grew up LOVING all things Christmas. But you'll know this already if you've listened to her holiday single, "Christmas Tree Farm." The music video contains super-sweet video clips of a very little Taylor, with her brother and parents, opening presents, sledding, and basically having lots of festive fun!

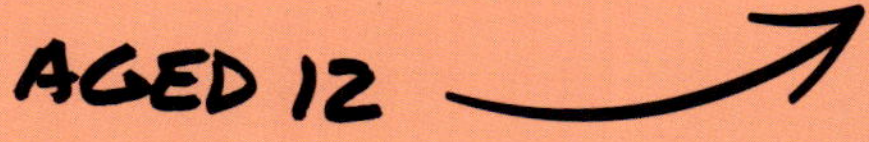

AGED 12

NASHVILLE

Nashville

Music was important to Taylor from a young age. She started out by singing covers in talent contests, but age at 12, she learned to play guitar and began writing her own songs. As a kid, Taylor REALLY wanted to move to Nashville in Tennessee, where famous country singers like Dolly Parton and Faith Hill had got their big breaks. Taylor was determined to succeed and would tirelessly send her demo tapes to different studios in the hope that someone would sign her.

Big Move

When she was 13 years old, Tay's family moved from Pennsylvania to Nashville so that she could follow her music-career dreams. Taylor soon nabbed herself a record deal with Big Machine Records. Just two years later, Taylor released her first album, called *Taylor Swift,* which included the song "Tim McGraw". This track went on to become her first top-40 hit as well as Breakthrough Video of the Year at the 2007 CMT Music Awards.

Fearless

A new level of success came for Taylor in 2008 as she scored her first No. 1 album with *Fearless*. That same year, she raised her profile by performing with the mega-popular Jonas Brothers on their Burnin' Up Tour.

JONAS BROTHERS

BIG WINS!

2010 saw Taylor's stardom zoom to new heights when she won big at the Grammys. And we mean BIG... Check it out:

- ★ **ALBUM OF THE YEAR - *Fearless***
- ★ **BEST FEMALE COUNTRY VOCAL PERFORMANCE**
- ★ **BEST COUNTRY SONG**
- ★ **BEST COUNTRY ALBUM**

Record Breaker

The iconic "We Are Never Ever Getting Back Together" from Taylor's fourth album, *Red*, is one of her most famous singles. In 2012 it broke the record as the fastest-selling digital single ever by a female artist. *Red* was also a big move away from TayTay's country sound.

NEW YORK

Big Apple

In 2014, Taylor left her beloved Nashville behind to move to the Big Apple—New York City. She released her dance-floor filler "Shake It Off," an unforgettable single from her fifth album *1989*. During her *1989* world tour, Taylor began to introduce famous guests appearances at her shows. Celebs included Lisa Kudrow (Phoebe from *Friends*), actress Julia Roberts, and Mick Jagger (lead singer of The Rolling Stones). The tour was mega and got everybody talking!

SHAKE IT OFF

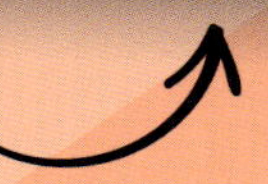

REPUTATION TOUR

Back With a Bang . . .

After a short break, Taylor came back better than ever (if you can imagine that!) in 2017 with the single "Look What You Made Me Do." It was from her sixth album, *Reputation*. By 2018 she left the record label Big Machine for Republic Records and Universal Music Group.

Loving It

Taylor released her seventh album, *Lover*, into the world in 2019. With 18 tracks, this was her longest to date. She released it in the same year that she appeared in the movie adaptation of Andrew Lloyd Webber's *Cats*. Is there nothing this gal can't do? In 2020, Taylor released *Folklore*, her eighth album, which nabbed her another Grammy for Album of the Year. Later that same year, she released her ninth album—*Evermore*.

GRAMMYS PERFORMANCE 2020

Late-Night Inspo

Taylor's tenth album, *Midnights*, was released in 2022 and has a synth-pop sound. Taylor says that it was inspired by sleepless nights and that she even wrote some of the songs in the middle of the night! Ten of the 13 songs occupied the entire top 10 of the US Billboard Hot 100 on its release.

The Tortured Poets Department

Swifties everywhere got an epic double-dose of Taylor when she dropped her longest ever album in April 2024.

11th Album

This is Taylor's 11th studio album, and she cowrote it with two producers. The first is Jack Antonoff (who she's worked with for 10 years!) and the second is Aaron Dessner (who coproduced her *Folklore* and *Evermore* albums).

Spotify Record

It became the first album ever on Spotify to get over 300 million streams in a single day!

New Era

Taylor added a new *Tortured Poets* section to her Eras Tour.

Cool Collaboration

We all love a cool collaboration, and when Taylor teams up with Florence Welch on her "Florida!!!" track, it's nothing short of magical. Does it make you want to belt it out at the top of your lungs too? What an anthem!

WINNING THE BEST COLLABORATION AWARD FOR "FORTNIGHT" AT THE 2024 MTV VIDEO MUSIC AWARDS.

Love Songs

TTPD is filled with poetry about love and loss. This is the first album that TayTay released since she began dating football player Travis Kelce of the Kansas City Chiefs. "The Alchemy" talks about the chemistry between her and Travis. Whereas the track "So Long, London" is thought to be about her ex-boyfriend Joe Alwyn.

★

Listen out for Tay's literary references (she's a big reader!) as well as icons such as singer-songwriter Patti Smith and Welsh poet Dylan Thomas.

The Anthology

Just when you thought things couldn't get any better, Taylor released a second version of the album, *The Tortured Poets Department: The Anthology*. This epic double album features 31 songs. The LP sold 1.4 million copies on its first day!

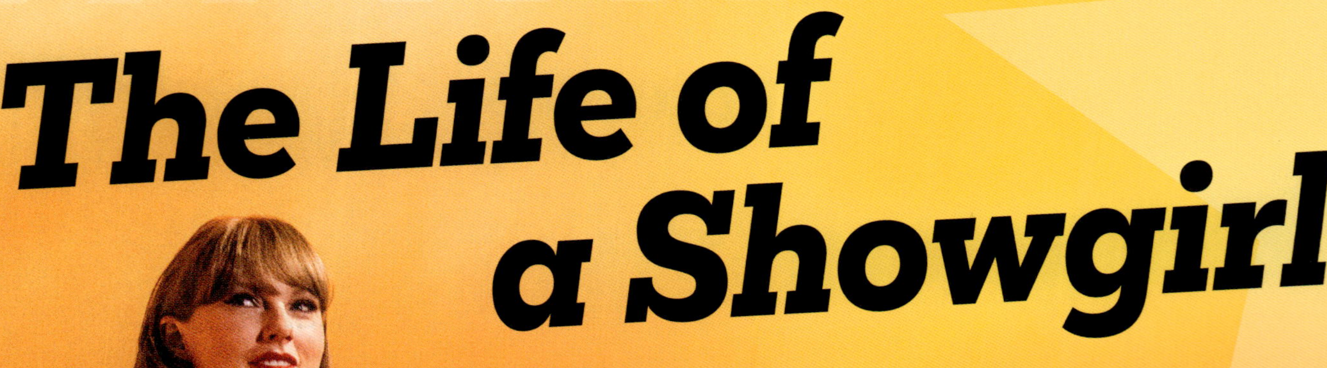

The Life of a Showgirl

Tay's latest release adds megawatt sunshine to that showgirl sparkle. Is this the pop star's most joyful album yet?

★★★★★★★★★★★★★★★★★★

Inspired by Eras

Tay wrote the songs on the album while on tour as her creative outlet. Between her 52 shows in Europe, she worked with Swedish legends Max Martin (pictured) and Shellback to produce it.

Podcast Debut

Tay made a big surprise announcement about her 12th album on her boyfriend Travis Kelce's podcast with his brother, New Heights. The two-hour episode broke the record for the most simultaneous views of a podcast on YouTube.

Trav Tracks

Many of the songs on the album—including "The Fate of Ophelia," "Opalite," and "Wi$h Li$t"—are about her boyfriend Travis, who proposed before its release.

Box-Office Hit

Taylor threw herself a release party at cinemas for the new album, topping the box office with more than $46 million in ticket sales over a three-day run.

Title Track

The last song on the album, "The Life of a Showgirl," is the ultimate "Taybrina" masterpiece. Taylor has shared the stage with Sabrina Carpenter many times, and this track sees the two friends dueting on the highs and lows of their fabulous showgirl lives.

The cover art of Tay in a bathtub is her modern remake of an 1852 painting of Ophelia, a character from the Shakespeare play *Hamlet*, who is referenced in the opening single.

Special Editions

In addition to the best-selling original, there are multiple deluxe variants of the album with different glam cover images and exclusive bonus content. Some fans set out to collect them all!

TAYLOR IN NUMBERS

12 ALBUMS RELEASED

"Anti-Hero" spent
8 WEEKS
AT **No.1** ON THE US BILLBOARD HOT 100

125 WEEKS
AT **No. 1** ON THE US BILLBOARD ARTIST 100 CHART

13 years old
AGE TAYLOR SIGNED WITH **her First Record Label**

Only artist
IN HISTORY TO WIN
ALBUM OF THE YEAR
FOR A **4th time**
AT THE 2024 GRAMMYS

40 AMERICAN MUSIC AWARDS RECEIVED

14 UK NO. 1 ALBUMS

280 MILLION + INSTAGRAM FOLLOWERS

19 YEARS OLD AGE TAYLOR BECAME THE YOUNGEST EVER COUNTRY MUSIC AWARDS **Entertainer of the Year**

35 YEARS OLD AGE TAYLOR BECAME THE **first female artist** TO SURPASS **100 MILLION** IN ALBUM SALES

33 UK TOP 10 SINGLES

Top Hits and Anthems

Let's celebrate some of Taylor's finest tunes, from her beautiful ballads to her "sick beats"—plus the songs that made her famous!

TIM MCGRAW

Album: **Taylor Swift**

Year: **2006**

We couldn't not mention this single. This is where it all began after all. This love song is classic Taylor, and it was her first top 10 country hit as well as her first US Billboard Hot 100 chart entry. Taylor was inspired to write this song when she was still at school.

LOVE STORY

Album: **Fearless**

Year: **2008**

When 17-year-old Taylor's parents didn't want her to date a guy, she channeled her frustration into writing this song. It has strong fairy tale vibes (princes and princesses, eat your hearts out!) and those famous lyrics about the forbidden love of Romeo and Juliet.

SHAKE IT OFF

Album: **1989**

Year: **2014**

This uber-catchy track has become a dance-floor favorite that's guaranteed to get everyone singing and bopping along, no matter who they are. It's the perfect track to rid yourself of negativity! The upbeat song was Taylor's second No. 1 hit.

BLANK SPACE

Album: **1989**

Year: **2014**

If it's bangers you're after, then look no further than *Blank Space*! This pop anthem kicks in with a strong beat that makes you want to jump up and sing along. The clever lyrics make fun of all the negative stories about Taylor's personal life in the media.

ANTI-HERO

Album: **Midnights**

Year: **2022**

This single is all about self-doubt and feeling insecure, and it totally dominated the charts. Taylor wrote this one with Jack Antonoff, and it went on to top the US Billboard Hot 100 for eight weeks, making it TayTay's longest running No. 1 hit... so far.

Following the release of her album *Midnights*, Taylor broke the record for the most top 10 hits by a female artist with an incredible 40 of them.

10 Reasons We Love Tay

There are SO many reasons, right? But we've whittled it down to our top 10.

1

FEMINIST ICON

Taylor isn't afraid to speak out about important issues, and feminism is close to her heart. She often shares love for fellow female artists—she's all about lifting people up.

2

DONATES TO CHARITY

From funding wildlife and conservation charities to donating her autographed guitar to PETA, Taylor spreads the word about charities she cares about.

3

SHOWS LOVE FOR FANS

Whether she's offering advice to them on social media or thanking them for her success, Taylor is constantly showing her fans the love and that she never takes them for granted!

DEDICATED CAT MOMMA

She is one proud cat parent to her beloved feline friends, and she takes them everywhere. More about her fur babies on page 20!

5

WRITES HER OWN SONGS

Not only does Taylor write her own chart-topping hits, but she writes them for other artists, too, like Calvin Harris.

DIRECTS MUSIC VIDEOS

The first music video Taylor directed was for her 2019 track, "The Man." This gal proves you really can do it all, and she bosses it every time!

7 SHE'S HONEST

Besides writing songs about her life and experiences, Taylor has also talked openly about being lonely and finding school tough because she didn't have many friends.

8 THE DANCE MOVES!

Taylor dances like nobody is watching. When she moves, it's all about having fun and not at all about trying to look cool! It's the best way.

9 HER FRIENDS ARE #SQUADGOALS

Yup, hands down, TayTay's got THE coolest girl gang, and we all want to be a part of it.

10 SHE IS GROUNDED

Even though she's one of the biggest popstars ever, Taylor hasn't let it go to her head. She still gets super excited about the things she gets to do!

Pet Corner

All you Swifties out there will know that TayTay has three fabulous and furry family members who she talks about . . . A LOT. Taylor takes her role as Cat Mom very seriously, and we're here for it. Get ready for cuteness overload!

CAT "SQUAD"

NAME: Meredith Grey
BREED: Scottish fold
ADOPTED: 2011
NAMED AFTER:
Meredith Grey from *Grey's Anatomy*

A SCOTTISH FOLD CAT

A SCOTTISH FOLD CAT

NAME: Olivia Benson
BREED: Scottish fold
ADOPTED: 2014
NAMED AFTER:
Olivia Benson from *Law and Order: SVU*

NAME: Benjamin Button
BREED: Ragdoll
ADOPTED: 2019
NAMED AFTER:
Benjamin Button in the movie of the same name

A RAGDOLL CAT

Both Ellen Pompeo, who played Meredith Grey in *Grey's Anatomy*, and Mariska Hargitay, who played Olivia Benson in *Law and Order: SVU*, appear in Taylor's "Bad Blood" music video.

Paw-fect Match

We met Benjamin when he appeared in Taylor's music video for "Me!" In fact, that's where Taylor met him too! It was love at first sight—Taylor adopted him, and the rest is history.

First-Class Passengers

Taylor's cats go everywhere with her, and they sure travel in style.

Career Kitty

It turns out Olivia has a career to rival any human's and has made it onto the 2023 Pet Rich List. From cameos in Taylor's music videos to a successful career in commercials, Olivia even has her own merch! So extra.

Plus Two

A-list events are a go for Meredith and Olivia, who were Tay's dates at the 2019 Billboard Music Awards. They really are living the dream!

The Squad

It's the team all Swifties dream of being part of—Taylor and her famous girl gang are absolute squad goals!

Gracie Abrams

This Swiftie grew up to become part of her idol's inner circle. A talented songwriter who has risen to pop fame, Gracie became close to Taylor while opening for her during the Eras Tour. As friends, they've made some sweet music together, including Gracie's Grammy-nominated single, "Us."

Emma Stone

The friendship began when they both attended the Young Hollywood Awards in 2008, where they hit it off. Since then, Tay has accompanied Emma to one of her movie premieres, and Emma has come along to some of Taylor's tours.

Lorde

Taylor sent flowers to Lorde when she released her first ever single, "Royals." This act of kindness led to them meeting up and becoming pals.

Gigi Hadid

This duo has been BFFs since they met at an event in 2014. Gigi was one of the pals featured in Taylor's famous "Bad Blood" music video. Gigi tries to make it to as many of Taylor's shows as she can and sometimes even joins Tay on stage.

Selena Gomez

This friendship started when Taylor and Selena were both dating Jonas brothers (Joe and Nick) in 2008. Although the relationships ended, the girls have stayed friends. Taylor has been to Selena's movie premieres, they hang out at awards shows together, and they've even sung together.

All About the Eras Tour

Tay's record-breaking tour took those fans who were lucky enough to get tickets through all of her musical eras, with songs from every studio album.

44 SONGS
IN THE SET LIST, TAKEN FROM **11 ALBUMS**
★★★★★★★★★★★★★★★★★★★★
WHICH REPRESENT THE **11 "ERAS" OF TAYLOR**

ERAS WAS THE **HIGHEST-GROSSING** TOUR OF **ALL TIME**, WITH MORE THAN
$2 billion
IN TICKET SALES

10,168,008
TICKETS SOLD OVER
149 shows

MARCH 2023
DATE THE **ERAS TOUR** DEBUTED IN THE US

TAYLOR'S FIRST TOUR SINCE THE **REPUTATION** STADIUM TOUR IN **2018**

Taylor sung TWO SURPRISE ACOUSTIC TRACKS DURING EACH SHOW

SHE OFTEN TREATED FANS TO A **SPECIAL GUEST** TO HELP WITH THIS PART

"I don't know how to process how you all are making me feel right now."

Taylor Swift on her opening night

Fans ♥ Taylor

When it comes to showing appreciation for her fans, Taylor does not hold back. Think surprise wedding appearances, handwritten letters, and love advice!

She sticks up for them

When TayTay saw a fan being yelled at by security at her concert, she stopped singing to defend them. The Swifties were just dancing, and for some reason, this security guard didn't like it. The security guard was then asked to leave, and the fan and her friends were given free tickets to the gig.

She writes her fans handwritten letters

Tay takes the time to reply to her fans with letters. And they're not just typed form letters either—they're personalized and handwritten. Even more special, they're often decorated with her beautiful watercolor paintings.

She shows up at their weddings

How could your big day get even bigger? Invite Taylor Swift. Yep, she turned up to surprise one of her superfans on their wedding day. Not only did Taylor sing her hit "Blank Space" while playing the piano, but she even painted the couple a watercolor card featuring the lyric "so it's gonna be forever."

SHE GIVES THEM ADVICE ON SOCIAL MEDIA

Lots of fans message their idols on Instagram never expecting their hero to see it, let alone reply. But Taylor isn't like most popstars! Over the years, she's thrilled fans with brilliant replies and helpful advice. Let's be honest, she's like the big sister we all want!

Cool Collabs

Just like all of Tay's musical decisions, her choice of artists to work with are always top-notch. Here are some of the A-listers that are proud to be Team Taylor.

Haim

This friendship has been a long-running one. Back in 2015, the Haim sisters joined Tay on her *1989* World Tour. They also collaborated on Taylor's 2020 *Evermore* album on the track called "No Body, No Crime." In 2022, Taylor joined the Haim girls at London's O2 Arena. Together the fierce foursome performed a mashup of "Love Song" from Taylor's *Fearless* album, along with a rendition of "Gasoline."

Lana Del Rey

Tay is always shouting about what a legend Lana Del Rey is, so it's no surprise she asked her to collaborate on 'Snow on the Beach', a beautiful track off *Midnights*. Tay even brought Lana as her date to the 2024 Grammy Awards where *Midnights* won Album of the Year.

Miley Cyrus

Taylor and Miley sang together at the 51st Grammys in 2009. The unstoppable gals belted out a stripped-back rendition of Taylor's song "Fifteen." Check it out for a throwback to old-school Taylor (and Miley too!), harmonies galore, and Taylor rocking it on her guitar.

Kendrick Lamar

In her infamous "Bad Blood" track, Taylor collaborated with hip-hop royalty, Kendrick Lamar. But before they got to this point, the pair had talked openly about how they admired one another's music and even shared videos singing or lip-syncing each other's songs. Love it!

Sir Paul McCartney

Taylor met with Sir Paul McCartney (of The Beatles) for *Rolling Stone* magazine in 2020, to talk about their music. It turns out that Taylor's relationship with her young fans inspired Paul McCartney's song, "Who Cares."

Ed Sheeran

Besides being good mates for a long time, Ed and Taylor enjoy making music together. Ed collaborated with Taylor on three of her songs: "Everything Has Changed" (*Red* album), "End Game" (*Reputation* album), and "Run" (*Red: Taylor's version*). Taylor was then on a remix of Ed's "The Joker and the Queen" track.

Taylor's Style Evolution

Looking good! Check out TayTay's fashion choices from cute curls and cowboy boots to bold blazers and bodysuits.

2009

BERET CHIC Keeping it cool and classic with a bold red beret and natural waves.

2006

COUNTRY CUTENESS

Throwback to the early days of Taylor sporting halters and cowboy boots.

BELLE OF THE BALL Giving off princess vibes at the Grammys in this lilac bodice.

2008

2016

MONOCHROME MINI

Now, that's how you make a statement—black lips, bleached hair, and a cut-out mini dress.

TARTAN TWO-PIECE Matching sets have become a signature Swift style!

TAILORED TAYLOR

Taylor looked the business in this super-luxe, velvet blazer.

FLOWER POWER

Bringing all the spring vibes with a floral explosion of a dress.

COLOR POP Going for bold with this graphic blazer with shoulder pads. Iconic!

BOHO BABE Big sleeves, pastel shades, and delicate floral detailing—what's not to love?

HOLLYWOOD GLAM

Long black gloves, a leg slit, and LAYERS of diamond necklaces. A red-carpet classic!

2024

QUIZ

What's Your Taylor Look?

Taylor's mastered heaps of awesome looks over the years, but which one is most you? Take this quiz and jot down your answers to reveal all.

1 **Pick a hairstyle:**

A. French plaits
B. Big, bouncy curls
C. Ringlets

2 **Pick an accessory:**

A. Flower crown
B. Gold bracelet and rings
C. Hoop earrings

3 **In a school play, you'd prefer to be...**

A. Making the costumes
B. Acting the main part
C. Playing a musical instrument

4 **You're choosing an outfit for a big event. Which kind of dress would you go for?**

A. Something feminine and floral
B. Anything with sequins
C. A cute halter

5 **What's your favorite way to spend a Saturday?**

A. Beach trip
B. Cinema
C. Country walk

6 **Your dream holiday would be a...**

- **A.** Fab festival
- **B.** City getaway
- **C.** Outdoor adventure

7 **Choose a weekend activity:**

- **A.** Reading a good book
- **B.** Going out on the town with my besties
- **C.** Writing music

8 **Which is your favorite subject at school?**

- **A.** Art
- **B.** Drama
- **C.** Music

9 **In your friendship group, you're the...**

- **A.** Listener
- **B.** Leader
- **C.** Chill one

10 **When you grow up, you'd rather be a...**

- **A.** Artist
- **B.** Movie star
- **C.** Musician

MOSTLY A's

Your Taylor style is BOHO BABE.

Teaming pretty, floaty dresses with your loose waves is your signature style, and the best part is that you make it look effortless! You love daisy chains, flower crowns, and ditsy detailing.

MOSTLY B's

Your Taylor style is HOLLYWOOD GLAM.

There's nothing low-key about your look, and that's why everyone loves it. It doesn't matter if you're going for a milkshake or dressing up for a party, you know how to bring silver-screen glamor to any outfit. Bring on the sparkly sequins and shine!

MOSTLY C's

Your Taylor style is COUNTRY CUTENESS.

You're happiest in denim, plaid, and casual halter dresses. This was Taylor's vibe when the world first caught a glimpse of her! Just like TayTay, whatever you wear, you always manage to put your own unique stamp on it. Cowboy boots for the win!

It's a Love Story...

Our girl has found her match, and we couldn't be happier for her. "Tayvis" forever!

Swift Facts

NAME:	Travis Michael Kelce
FROM:	Westlake, Ohio
DATE OF BIRTH:	5 October 1989 (the same year as Tay!)
JOB:	Pro football player for the Kansas City Chiefs

★

"Everything this man touches turns into happiness and fun and magic."

Tay on Trav

Calling on the Megaphone

Travis famously announced on his hit podcast New Heights that he had gone to see the Eras Tour in his place of work, the Kansas City Chiefs' Arrowhead Stadium, and was sad that he was unable to give Taylor a friendship bracelet with his number on it. Looks like Taylor got the message afterall!

Breaking the Internet

When Tay & Trav announced their engagement in a joint Insta post in August 2025, it quickly broke the repost record and sent the internet into a frenzy. The classic caption read: "Your English teacher and your gym teacher are getting married."

Travis popped the question with a 10-carat dazzler in his backyard, which he had sneakily turned into a fairytale rose garden. As Tay said: "10/10."

Why Swifties like Trav...

- He's kind.
- He's genuine.
- He's hilarious.
- He's super supportive of Tay's career.
- He gives her the undying admiration she deserves.
- He makes Taylor feel more able to express her true self.
- He's happy to share their happiness.
- It has to be a sign that when you combine their lucky numbers (87 + 13), it equals 100%.
- He loves Swifties!

SWIFTIES CELEBRATE THE CHIEFS' SUPER BOWL VICTORY IN FEBRUARY 2024. TAY IS CREDITED WITH GETTING MORE GIRLS INTERESTED IN FOOTBALL.

TayTay's Trophy Case

Nobody can deny that this country-turned-pop singer rocks the awards season each year. Here are some of her biggest wins to date and counting . . .

15x MTV EUROPE AWARDS

FOR 2022 ALONE, TAY WON . . .

- ★ Best Video and Best Longform Video for "All Too Well" (10 Minute Version)
- ★ Best Artist ★ Best Pop

Taylor is tied with Drake for the most wins at the BILLBOARD MUSIC AWARDS with 39 each.

39x BILLBOARD MUSIC AWARDS

- ★ Top Artist **2013, 2015, and 2023**
- ★ Top Selling Album **2018**
- ★ Top Country Album for her version of *Red* **2022**

23x MTV VIDEO MUSIC AWARDS

- "Bad Blood" **2015**
- "You Need to Calm Down" **2019**
- "All Too Well" (10 Minute Version) **2021**

In 2023, Tay went from 14 VMAs to 23.

NICKELODEON KIDS' CHOICE AWARDS

FOR 2023 ALONE, TAY WON . . .

- Favorite Female Artist
- Favorite Album for *Midnights (3am Edition)*

Taylor's cat **OLIVIA BENSON** was named 2023 Favorite Celebrity Pet

NICKELODEON KIDS' CHOICE AWARDS

14x GRAMMY AWARDS

HIGHLIGHTS INCLUDE . . .

- Album of the Year (for *Fearless, 1989* and *Folklore*)
- Best Music Video (for "Bad Blood")
- Best Female Country Vocal Performance (for "White Horse")

40x AMERICAN MUSIC AWARDS

HIGHLIGHTS INCLUDE . . .

- Favorite Country Female Artist
- Artist of the Decade **2019**
- Artist of the Year **2020**

5 YEARS IN A ROW!

Favorite Country Female Artist

AMERICAN MUSIC AWARDS

8 songs You Didn't Know Were By Taylor

As if the back catalog of her own hits aren't enough, Taylor has been writing for movies and major artists, too!

Hannah Montana (movie)

Miley sang "You'll Always Find Your Way Back Home" in the 2009 movie *Hannah Montana: The Movie*. But you may not know that it was written by Taylor Swift along with a singer called Martin Johnson. Taylor also put in a star performance in the movie when she sang "Crazier."

Sugarland

The American country music duo, Sugarland, have a song called "Babe" that was written by Taylor and Patrick Monahan.

Little Big Town

"Better Man" was released by Little Big Town in 2016, and it was a huge hit—so huge that it even won Song of the Year at the Country Music Awards in 2017. The country band have a lot to thank Taylor for, seeing as she wrote the song and sent it to them. Taylor also sings the song on her album *Red (Taylor's Version)*.

Calvin Harris

Remember that Calvin Harris banger "This Is What You Came For?" The song featured Rihanna and was written by Taylor when she and Calvin were dating. The pair chose to keep this on the down-low as they thought it could be a distraction for fans.

Hunger Games (movie)

Along with The Civil Wars band, Tay co-wrote "Safe and Sound" from the *Hunger Games* movie soundtrack. Besides this track, one of Taylor's own songs, "Eyes Open," made its way onto the movie soundtrack.

Boys Like Girls

Taylor wrote "Two Is Better Than One" with singer-songwriter Martin Johnson for his band Boys Like Girls.

Big Red Machine

Taylor teamed up with The National / Big Red Machine's Aaron Dessner to write the track "Renegade". She also sings on the song!

Cats (the movie)

It's no surprise that a cat obsessive like TayTay would want to get involved with the *Cats* movie. Not only did she star in it as a feline called Bombalurina, but she also co-wrote the movie's theme song "Beautiful Ghosts" with Andrew Lloyd Webber.

Our 5 Favorite Music Videos

It's hard to choose a top 5 from all of Tay's outstanding offerings, but we managed it!

BEST DANCE MOVES

You Belong With Me

(from the album *Fearless*)

There's a lot to love about this one. It's fun, it's endearing, and it's all about championing the underdog. It's that classic teen romcom set-up with cheerleaders versus nerds, love notes galore, and even a prom! Taylor plays two parts—the nerd who dances like nobody's watching, plus the popular girl with the car and boyfriend. The main message is to embrace your inner nerd and don't change to be liked.

Bad Blood (from the album *1989*)

This notorious music video has a big celeb ensemble, like seriously BIG. We're talking about Zendaya, Hailee Steinfeld, Cara Delevingne, Kendrick Lamar, Cindy Crawford, Karlie Kloss, and Selena Gomez to name but a few. When this song comes on, you wake up and pay attention! The video has stunts aplenty, which the multi-talented Taylor performed herself.

BEST CAMEOS!

BEST STORYTELLING

Blank Space (from the album *1989*)

Released in 2015, "Blank Space" was co-written by Taylor and is set in an epic mansion. We love her costumes, her ace acting skills, and then there's the beautiful white horses. And of course, her cat Olivia makes an appearance. Taylor's storytelling skills shine bright in this video, which is bursting with drama and has over three billion views on YouTube. It also won MTV Video Music Awards for Best Female Video and Best Pop Video.

MOST BEAUTIFUL

Wildest Dreams

(from the album *1989*)

We cannot talk about this video without mentioning the stunning setting. It was filmed in Africa, with amazing lions, giraffes, and beautiful waterfalls. The song is about remembering the good things in a relationship after it ends. In the video, Taylor is a glamorous fifties actress on a movie set. Oh, and THAT yellow dress? It's everything.

BEST COSTUMES AND CHOREOGRAPHY

The Fate of Ophelia

(from the album *The Life of a Showgirl*)

Sequins, feathers, fringes, and crystals galore—Tay went all-out for this absolute showstopper. Not only does she seamlessly shift between scenes embodying various glittering showgirls through the decades, she brings her entire cast of dancers from the Eras Tour along for the glamorous ride. What a reunion! Taylor wrote and directed this tour-de-force, which begins with her emerging from the Friedrich Heyser painting, *Ophelia*, wearing a flowing ivory gown. Leave it to Tay to give her millions of fans a lesson in art history as she dances away from the role of tragic heroine.

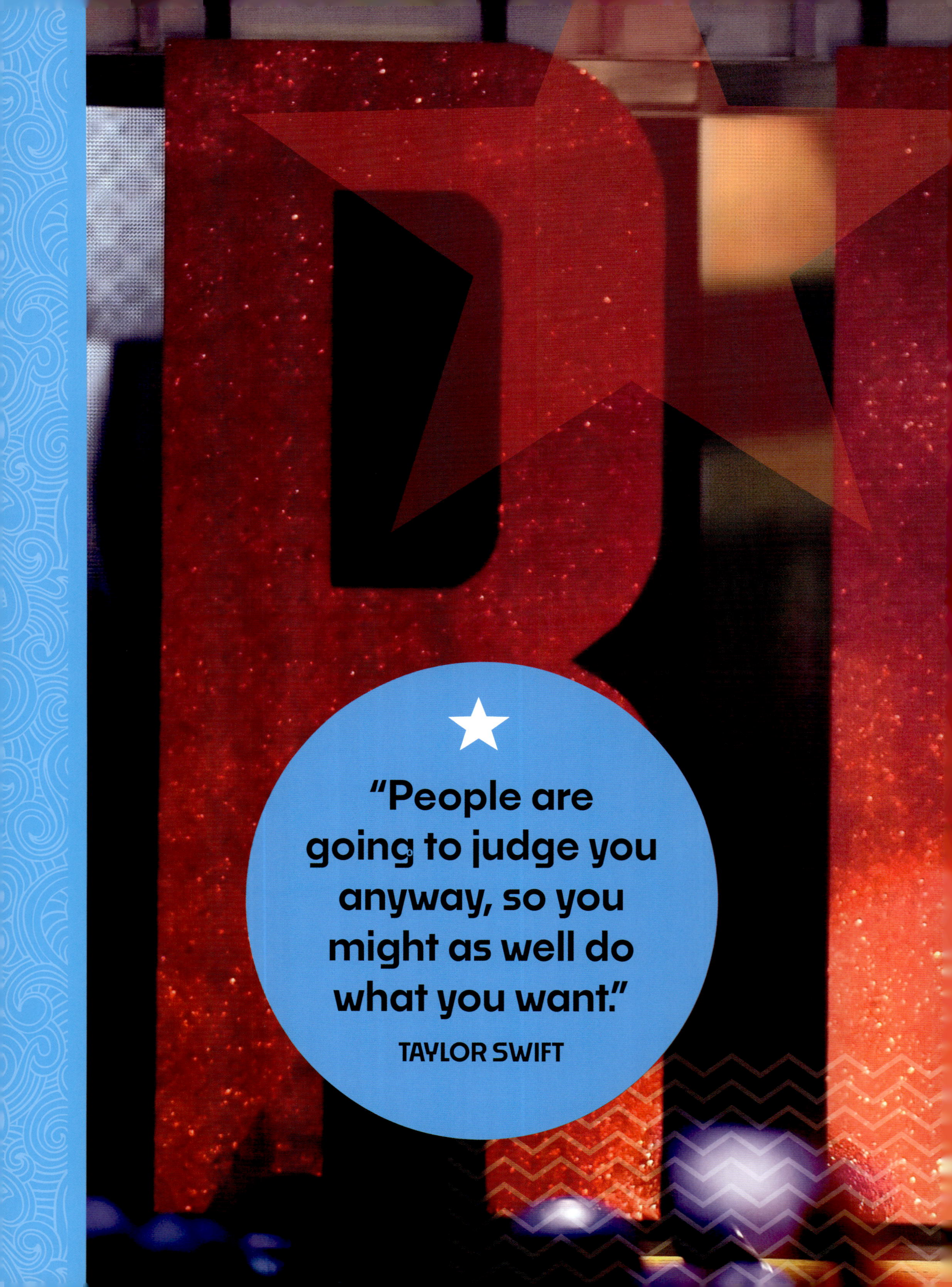
"People are going to judge you anyway, so you might as well do what you want."
TAYLOR SWIFT

10 Things You Didn't Know About Taylor

Read on and impress your crew with your super-Swiftie know-how.

She's still BFFs with Abigail—the friend mentioned in "Fifteen," remember?

2

Ten-year-old Taylor wrote a poem called "Monster In My Closet" and won a national poetry contest.

Tay was a model for Abercrombie & Fitch in 2003, just like Jennifer Lawrence, Emma Roberts, and Channing Tatum.

Taylor was taught to play guitar by a computer repairman.

TayTay's favorite TV show is *Friends.*

Horse-riding was a big part of Taylor's childhood. She competed until she was 12 years old.

We all know Tay writes her own songs, but she wrote the entire *Speak Now* album totally solo—not even one co-writer in sight!

8 She's named after American singer-songwriter James Taylor. This legendary guitarist has won six Grammys and is one of the best-selling artists of all time.

9 Taylor's grandmother, Marjorie, was an opera singer. Tay even wrote a song called "Marjorie" for her.

Tay paints a 13 on her hand before every show she plays. It's her lucky number and for good reasons—she was born on 13 December, her first album went gold in 13 weeks, and she was once sat in row 13 when she won an award.

We're Hair For It!

Let's take time to reflect on some highlights of Taylor's golden tresses.

Who remembers this super sweet look? Back in 2006, fresh-faced Taylor had a head of bouncy blonde waves.

We love this sophisticated style. Tay looks all kinds of elegant with this up-do!

Taylor was all about the Hollywood glamor with her fifties-style curls for this memorable MTV Music Awards' performance in 2010.

Blunt bangs has become one of Taylor's signature hairstyles! We love her 2013 full fringe with long locks.

Bob + side-swept bangs = volume! What's not to love?

Looking sharp at the 2016 Grammys with this blunt bob and soft bangs combo.

Hands up who loved Tay's bleach-blonde shaggy crop!

Could she look any edgier? TayTay glows with beautiful highlights and soft waves.

Check out Taylor's Abba-style feathered bangs. Obsessed.

This simple, sophisticated style screams, "Taylor means business" . . . although when doesn't she, right?

11 Signs You're a Taylor Superfan

Calling all Swifties . . . how many of these sound like you?

1. You know every single word to every single one of her songs.

2. Like all true fans, you've sent her fan mail. We all know how Taylor loves receiving letters!

3. She inspired you to write. You keep a diary and jot down poems or songs about your life, what you do and how you feel.

4. You can name all the members of her squad. All of them! A pal of Taylor's is a pal of yours.

5. If you overhear someone singing her lyrics incorrectly, you HAVE to correct them!

6. Whenever you hum a tune, it's guaranteed to be one of TayTay's.

7. You follow her pets' careers closely.

8 You took guitar lessons so you could be more like your hero.

9 Your jewelry box is filled with friendship bracelets from fellow Swifties.

10 You can hunt down all her Easter eggs without even consulting a guide.

11 If Tay says she likes an artist or group, you go give them a listen. No questions asked!

How to Write Songs the Swift Way

The songstress has shared many tips about her songwriting process over the years. Here's what we've learned...

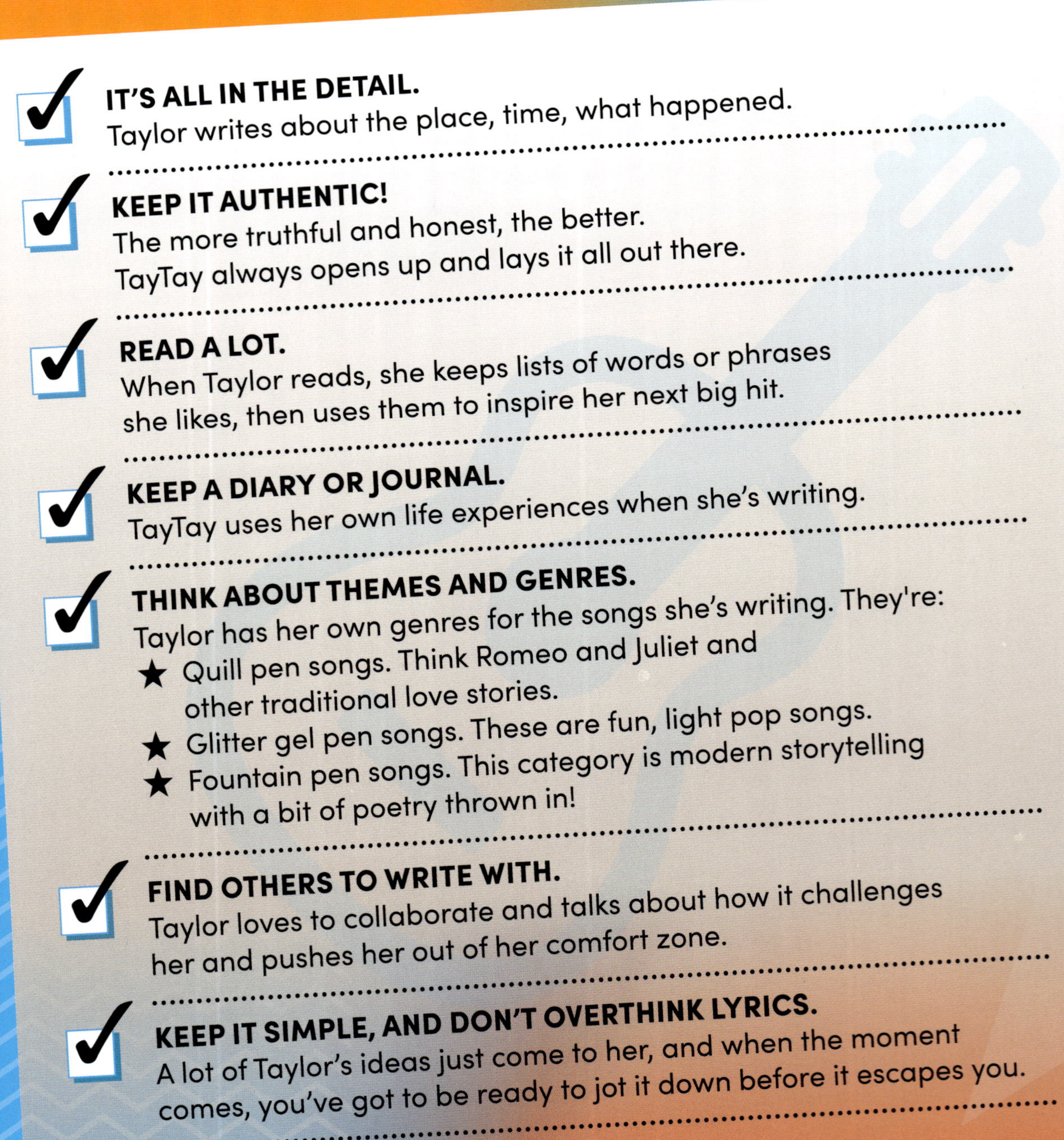

- **IT'S ALL IN THE DETAIL.**
  Taylor writes about the place, time, what happened.
- **KEEP IT AUTHENTIC!**
  The more truthful and honest, the better. TayTay always opens up and lays it all out there.
- **READ A LOT.**
  When Taylor reads, she keeps lists of words or phrases she likes, then uses them to inspire her next big hit.
- **KEEP A DIARY OR JOURNAL.**
  TayTay uses her own life experiences when she's writing.
- **THINK ABOUT THEMES AND GENRES.**
  Taylor has her own genres for the songs she's writing. They're:
  - ★ Quill pen songs. Think Romeo and Juliet and other traditional love stories.
  - ★ Glitter gel pen songs. These are fun, light pop songs.
  - ★ Fountain pen songs. This category is modern storytelling with a bit of poetry thrown in!
- **FIND OTHERS TO WRITE WITH.**
  Taylor loves to collaborate and talks about how it challenges her and pushes her out of her comfort zone.
- **KEEP IT SIMPLE, AND DON'T OVERTHINK LYRICS.**
  A lot of Taylor's ideas just come to her, and when the moment comes, you've got to be ready to jot it down before it escapes you.

"Writing songs is my life's work, my hobby, and my never-ending thrill. I am moved beyond words that you, my peers, decided to honor me in this way for work I'd still be doing if I had never been recognized for it."

TAYLOR SWIFT

"Know the person you are writing the songs about . . .Then write a letter to them—what you would say if you could? That's why I listen to music. It says how I feel better than I could. And it says what I wished I had said when that moment was there."

TAYLOR SWIFT

QUIZ

How Well Do You Know Tay?

Call yourself a Swiftie? Grab a pen and some paper and get ready to test your Taylor knowledge!

1 What is Taylor's lucky number?

2 Which member of Taylor's family was an opera singer?

3 Name Taylor's first album.

4 What is Taylor's favorite TV show?

5 What instrument did Taylor learn to play when she was 12?

6 Which album did Taylor write entirely by herself?

7 What type of farm did Taylor grow up on?

8 What single became Taylor's first top 40 hit?

9 Name all three of her cats.

10 What movie did Taylor write "You'll Always Find Your Way Back Home" for?

11 How old was Taylor when she wrote the poem "Monster In My Closet"?

12 Which movie did Taylor play a cat called Bombalurina in?

13 Where did Taylor and her family move to when she was 13?

ANSWERS:
1. 13, 2. GRANDMOTHER, MARJORIE, 3. *TAYLOR SWIFT*, 4. *FRIENDS*, 5. GUITAR, 6. *SPEAK NOW*, 7. CHRISTMAS TREE FARM, 8. "TIM MCGRAW", 9. MEREDITH GREY, OLIVIA BENSON, AND BENJAMIN BUTTON, 10. *HANNAH MONTANA: THE MOVIE*, 11. 10 YEARS OLD, 12. *CATS*, 13. NASHVILLE

Silver-Screen Star

As if dominating the music world wasn't enough, TayTay has also been a shining star in the film industry. Here are some of her starring roles... so far!

Hannah Montana: The Movie 2009

Taylor performed an original song called "Crazier" in this movie starring the one and only Miley Cyrus. Taylor's other songwriting cred on the soundtrack: "You'll Always Find Your Way Back Home."

The Lorax 2012

In this animation of Dr Seuss' *The Lorax*, Taylor voiced a teenager called Audrey. Zac Efron was another famous voice in the movie. He played teenager Ted.

Valentine's Day 2010

Starring as Felicia alongside *Twilight*'s Taylor Lautner, this movie was Taylor's first acting role in a feature film. The two Taylors played characters who were boyfriend and girlfriend on screen, and then the stars began dating in real life, earning their cute coupling the nickname "Taylor Squared." Taylor's song on the soundtrack: "Today Was a Fairytale."

The Giver 2014

Taylor's role may be small in this adaptation of Lois Lowry's book of the same name, but her musical talent is showcased in flashbacks, where she's playing the piano.

Cats 2019

Taylor played a furry feline in the movie adaptation of Sir Andrew Lloyd Webber's musical *Cats*. She perfected a British accent for her character Bombalurina, and delivered her song about the infamous bad cat, Macavity, while lying on a floating, sparkly moon. Taylor's song on the soundtrack: "Beautiful Ghost."

All Too Well 2021

Taylor wrote and directed this short movie, which is accompanied by her song of the same name. Multi-tasking and multi-talented TayTay also plays a supporting role in the movie—an older version of the character played by *Stranger Things* star Sadie Sink.

Amsterdam 2022

Swift is part of the star-studded cast of *Amsterdam*, appearing with the very talented Christian Bale, John David Washington, and Margot Robbie.

Other times Taylor features on movie soundtracks:
"Carolina"
for ***Where the Crawdads Sing***
"Safe and Sound"
for ***The Hunger Games***
"Message in a Bottle"
and **"Bad Blood"**
for ***DC League of Super-Pets***

"No matter what happens in life, be good to people. Being good to people is a wonderful legacy to leave behind."

TAYLOR SWIFT

Fan Guide

Want to be Taylor's No. 1 fan?
Here's how you do it.

1. Set yourself a challenge to learn all the lyrics to your fave Taylor songs.

2. Share your love of Taylor with your pals. We're sure they won't need much convincing! You could even start up your own fan club.

3. Put some pics of her up on your bedroom wall. Don't own any? Grab some paper and pens and create your own.

4. Listen to Tay's music in order, starting with her first album *Taylor Swift.* This may take some time since there are 12 of them!

5. Give writing your own songs a try. Taylor was writing for a long time before the world knew who she was.

6. Always big up your friends when they do well, rather than getting jealous about their success.

7. Make up a dance routine to your favorite song. Make sure you get your pals involved, too.

8. Send Taylor some fan mail (just in case you haven't already!). You never know—she may just write back!

9. Learn as many facts about Taylor as you can—this book is an excellent place to start.

10. At your next sleepover, treat yourself and your pals to one of her movies and plenty of popcorn.

11. Be more Taylor and surprise your family, friends, and neighbors with random acts of kindness. You could write them a handwritten letter or bake cookies for them.

12. And last, but not least, lend this book to a fellow Swiftie. Not only is it a kind thing to do, but it also means you'll have someone to talk all things Taylor with. Just make sure they give it back!

Doing Good

From donating to food banks to supporting disaster relief efforts, Tay reminds us all of the importance of standing up for what you believe in.

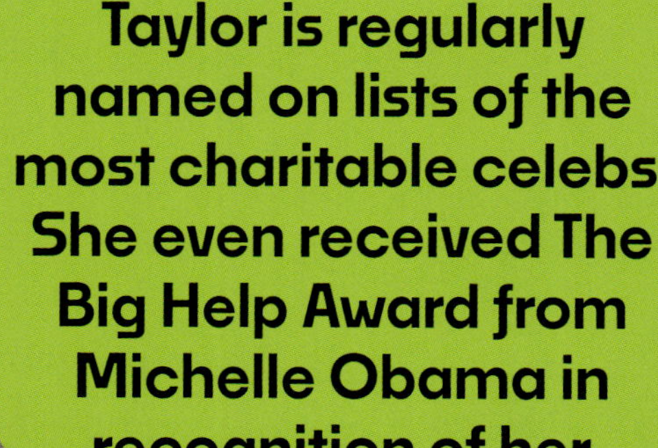

Taylor is regularly named on lists of the most charitable celebs. She even received The Big Help Award from Michelle Obama in recognition of her generosity.

GIVING BACK

From the Heart

Taylor has backed a huge variety of campaigns and charities over the years. She's partnered with UNICEF to help expand access to clean water, given millions to hurricane relief, funded the arts and education, and posted surprise life-changing donations to people in need.

Food Banks

While on The Eras tour, Swift made anonymous donations to food banks in every city she visited.

Wildlife Conservation

Taylor made sure money from her 'Wildest Dreams' music video went to African Parks Foundation of America. When she wore a vintage Monterey Bay Aquarium tee, she sparked a campaign that raised millions for sea otters.

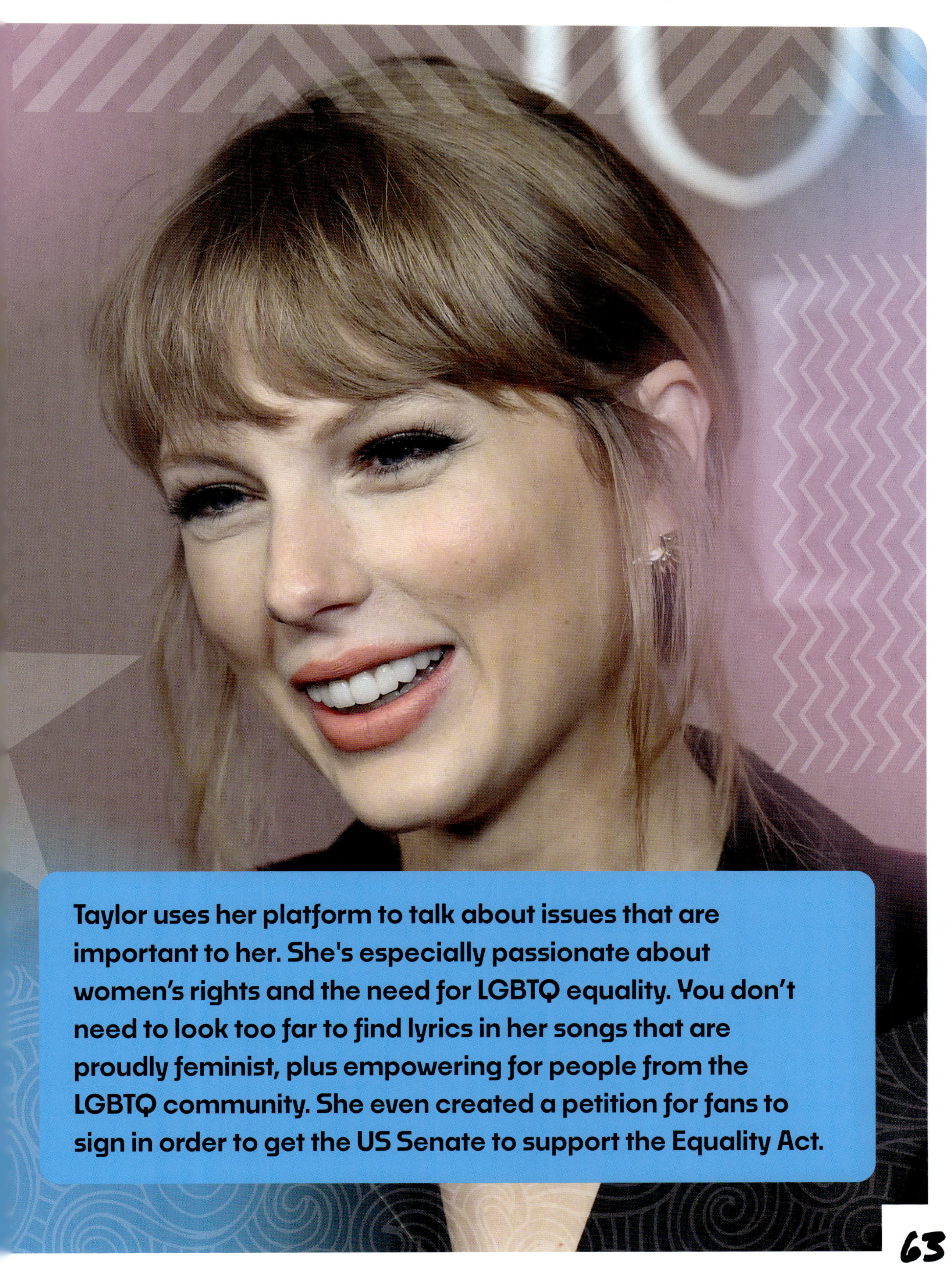

Taylor uses her platform to talk about issues that are important to her. She's especially passionate about women's rights and the need for LGBTQ equality. You don't need to look too far to find lyrics in her songs that are proudly feminist, plus empowering for people from the LGBTQ community. She even created a petition for fans to sign in order to get the US Senate to support the Equality Act.

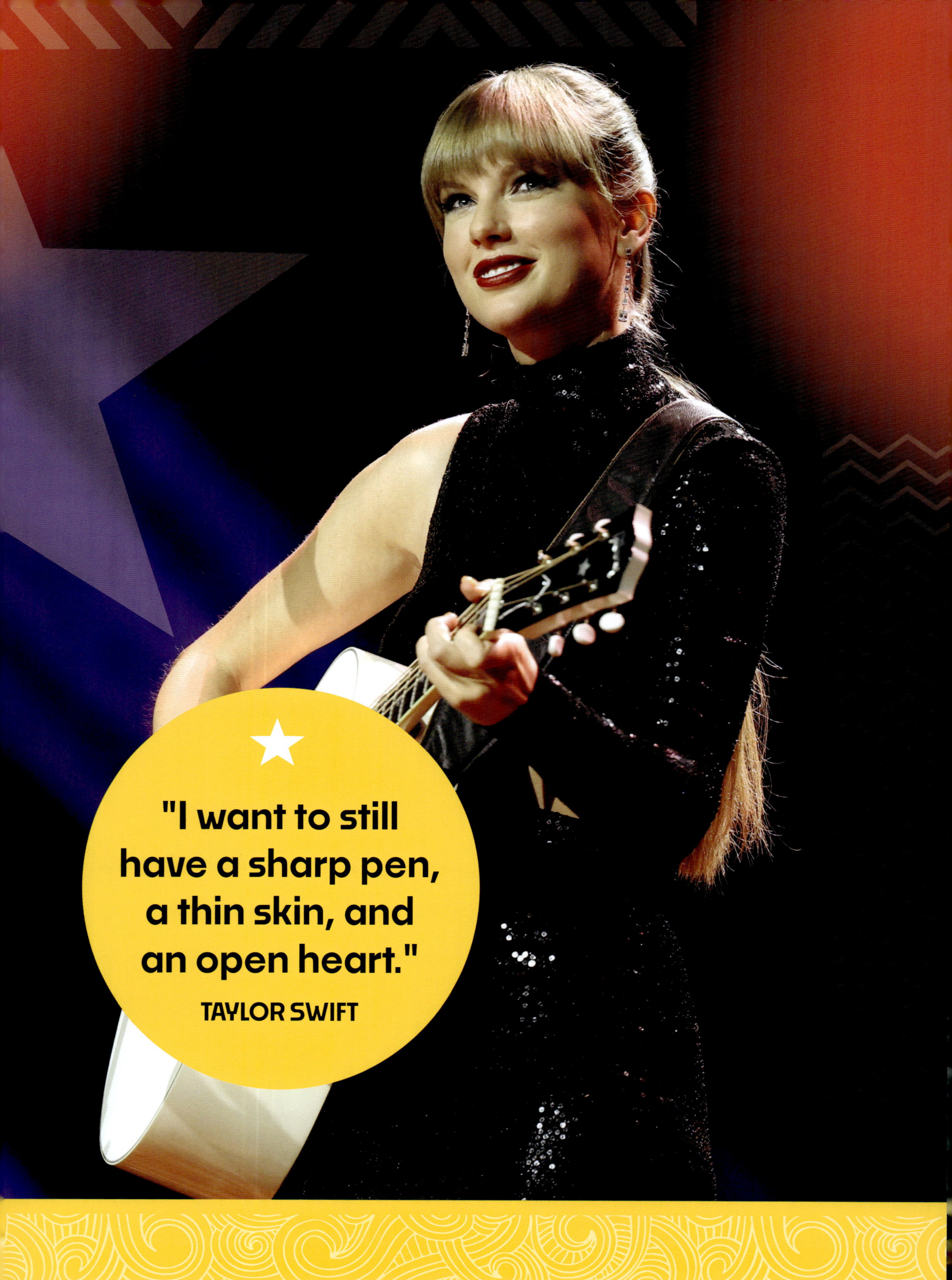
"I want to still have a sharp pen, a thin skin, and an open heart."
TAYLOR SWIFT